Journey into Paradise From the Hell of Afghanistan

M. Haroon Monis

Journey into Paradise from the Hell of Afghanistan
Copyright © 2007 by Haroon Monis

Summary: A family sets off on a journey to find freedom. They leave all their
livelihood behind and scale one of the world's most dangerous mountains
beyond which lies the hope for freedom—the beginning of a new life. But the
perils they face are here and now in front of them as the family tries *to
Journey into Paradise from the Hell of Afghanistan.*
[1. Nonfiction.   2. Autobiography.   3. Memoir   4. Culture/Heritage
5. Adoption—Nonfiction]   I. Title.

ISBN: 978-1-4303-1445-5

First Edition

Cover design by Milan Patel

Printed in the United States of America.

Foreword

As I was writing this novella, I never envisioned that its publication would be as troublesome as it has been. In trying to get this book to the audience it has so longingly awaited, I have discovered that there are so many people whose generosity and aid goes into making a product like this. I would like to take the space here to thank them.

Friendship becomes almost a sacred word when I use it calling the following people by it. Milan and Ashna are not just friends; they are saviors. There have been so few people who have helped me as much as these two. I love both of you and am indebted to both of you. Personally, I think that next to the definition *friend* your pictures should appear in the dictionary.

My love for the English language has been—in great regards—due to my wonderful teachers of English. As I think back, there are three that stand out. Mrs. Susan Noriega, my ESL teacher who planted the seeds of the English language in me; Dr. Carlotta Dwyer, who made English in high school be tough enough to prepare me for college; and Mr. Eric Mallin, my mentor and support system at University of Texas at Austin who taught me that it is okay to have views that go against the masses; it is okay to state your thoughts without fearing what those who have not quite thought the same thing might see as a result.

In their own way each one of these teachers put a positive spin on my life when I needed it. I am quite appreciative, and not a day goes by where I take for granted what they have enabled me to achieve.

There are also other teachers who have helped me, and I appreciate all of my teachers' help.

Last, but certainly not least, I would like to thank the members of my family who believed in my dreams and gave me the encouragement to do what made me happy. Thank you all so much.

~ Chapter One ~

The Escape Begins

Recently, since I am a schoolteacher, I did an activity with my students that was called, *Who Knew*? The purpose of the activity is to help students get to know each other better. I used myself as an example. On a sheet of paper I wrote four truths and a lie about myself and they were supposed to guess which the lie was. By doing this, many kids reveal sometimes funny, sometimes embarrassing things about themselves without much hesitation. I was no exception to the rule as I revealed some weird as well as tragic facts about myself. The five things I wrote down on the sheet of paper that I showed to my students were:

1. I have traveled halfway around the world.

2. As a child I used to jump out the window of a two-story house using an umbrella as a parachute.

3. A bus hit me when I was nine years old and I spent three weeks in a coma as well as three months in a cast because of a broken femur.

4. I have a bullet lodged in the back of my leg from when I got caught in the midst of gunfire between the Rebels and the Soviet backed soldiers in Afghanistan.

5. I have stood in two countries at the same time.

I write these down now as an introduction to all of you who read this book to simply show you that I have lived a life that a child should not witness. Have you guessed yet what the lie is among the five statements above? The lie is the statement that is numbered 4. However, that lie is not that far from the truth I do know.

As a young boy when I lived in Afghanistan, I saw war and savagery every day of my life. The truth about the statement that I have told you is false is that my older brother actually has endured that. I will tell you about that in a little bit.

I come from a large family. I am the last of eleven children born to a father who was educated and made his wealth based on his wits. He used the summer heat of the northern province of Afghanistan as a tool for making money. He opened an ice-making factory that made the Monis family a small fortune. One of the reasons I can sit here and tell this story is because we were wealthy and we could afford the hefty price tag one had to pay in order to be smuggled out of Afghanistan.

Because of the events of the 9-11 Attacks and the subsequent Operation Enduring Freedom, Afghanistan has been thrust into the American media spotlight. But the majority of Americans don't know about the years of war that the Afghans have endured. There has been fighting going on in that country since 1978. I was born in the capital, Kabul, in 1976, and all I knew was war just like all the Afghans. But the Monis family was staunchly opposed to the Communist regime that was trying so hard to gain control of Afghanistan. I had seen the problems with being opposed to the government first-hand. That was the reason Father planned for us to leave the country. Escape was not easy and would take a while. Additionally, given the size of the family, priority had to be given to those men in the family who were in danger of being drafted to fight in a war they didn't believe in.

At this point is where my oldest brother, Nadir, enters the picture. He had left Afghanistan before all this chaos—Russian invasion and the ensuing war—within Afghanistan had started. He had come to the U.S. in search of a more superior Western education. Given all the events that took place in that country, like the invasion of the Russians and the subsequent years of fighting, he knew he would be in America for the rest of his life. Thus, he was the one who suggested to Father that the rest of us might as well come to the U.S.

At this point in the seventh year of the war in Afghanistan, the draft age was 18-25. One of my brothers fell into that age range, Baryalai. When the soldiers would come to search our house for males to draft, he would sometimes hide in the closet, and at other times he would go up to the roof to avoid them. But we all knew that he would not be safe. So he was the first to leave Afghanistan after the country was embroiled in war. Father arranged for him to be smuggled out by a smuggler he found through some of his friends. The price was 15,000 Afghani Rupees. To put this money into the dollar terms would mean nothing. Therefore, I want to tell you what the average worker earned in a year. The average worker in Afghanistan earned about 25,000 to 35,000 rupees a year. So as you can see it is almost one year's salary to leave the country. As many as six million Afghans have actually been able to leave the country to date; some are now returning to their

7

homeland since there seems to be a more hopeful outlook on the horizon for Afghanistan.

Baryalai's destination would be Pakistan, which neighbors Afghanistan to the south and east. Father provided my brother, Barry, with enough money to be able to do something in Pakistan as far as earning a living was concerned. My older brother, Nadir, would try to find a way to get Barry into the U.S. Thus, Barry left Afghanistan, but the plight of the Monis family had just begun. We would be under more scrutiny from the government. The draft age was changed to include all males between 16 and 35 years of age because of the toll the war was taking on the Afghans. This put two more of my brothers in the age range for the draft.

~ Chapter Two ~

The Second Escape

Father once again scampered to find someone to get out these two brothers of mine to the safety of Pakistan. However, disaster was about to strike before he could get them out.

On a sunny afternoon in the middle of the fall of 1986, my brother Hamayoon was hanging out with a few friends on the side of the street. They had just purchased some roasted peanuts and some other dried fruit that they planned on eating as they stood and had a conversation.

I was playing marbles with a few of the neighborhood kids. Hamayoon did not let me hang out with his friends because I was a little kid, and they were older and thus better than me and my friends were. They told me that I was a little pest and that I needed to leave them alone.

Suddenly a group of soldiers showed up out of nowhere. Within minutes my brother's and his friends' identification cards were checked, and they were escorted into the dark green Hummer that the soldiers had arrived in. My brother had just been drafted for the war.

I walked into the house and told Mom what had just happened. Tears welled up in her eyes, and she told me I should have done something. I got confused because there was nothing I could do. She was hysterical. Seeing her hysteria, I cried too. We held each other, and tried to find comfort in the solace of being a strong family.

That night the Monis household was quiet. The electricity went out as it did every other night because the Afghan government had to conserve money for the war. I don't recall many nights when the electricity actually was on in the neighborhood. I usually studied by the light of the kerosene lamp. Our family had four of them.

That night after the fact that Hamayoon had been drafted, the lamp's dull glow almost seemed to make the mood of the Monis family members more melancholy. We needed some kind of resolve.

"Where have they taken him?" I asked Father who had returned a few hours ago from the Afghan marketplace known as The Bazaar.

"We don't know yet."

My brother Saleh, who had already served his three years in the Afghan Army, said to Father, "I have done my service, and I am not at risk of being drafted again any time soon. If you want, I can go try and find him and bring him back. But as soon as he comes back, we must have a place for him to go."

Saleh and Father decided that night that he would go to the province where they had taken my brother, Hamayoon. As soon as he returned to Kabul, Father would ship Hamayoon off to Pakistan.

By now, Barry, who had gone to Pakistan, had been able to gain asylum into the U.S.

We found out that Hamayoon had been assigned to the province of Logar, which was about 100 or so miles southwest of Kabul. Saleh set off for that province immediately, and a week later he returned with Hamayoon. But the weird thing was that when they entered our house in Kabul, it was Hamayoon who was carrying Saleh.

I was the one who opened the door to our house. Saleh looked kind of bad. His clothes were bloodstained. He seemed to have lost a lot of blood during the trip from Logar to Afghanistan. Hamayoon was also affected—he was pale, grim, and quieter than usual. Of course everyone grilled him on what had happened.

"As Saleh and I made our escape, there was a battle that erupted. The Rebels were moving onto the military base. The soldiers responded to fire by fire," as he spoke, his eyes were fierce as though he were reliving the most terrible event in his life. Thinking back, it must have been the most terrible thing he had seen in his young age—he was only 16 years old at this time.

"We were caught in the middle of the fire between the two sides. Since Saleh was behind me as he led me to the clearing, he caught the bullet that was intended for me," tears were rolling down Hamayoon's face. "This is all my fault that this happened to Saleh."

There was an initial hush in the dark room, as only silhouetted shadows tried to console my young brother, but finally Father spoke, "It is not your fault. He'll be fine." Don't blame yourself."

We had to hurry to save Saleh. Father sent for help. One of our family friends was a doctor. But as was the case with most families in Afghanistan, neither he nor we had a phone. Those who did have phones were not able to use it often either because a part of the war tactic was to cut out phone lines to cities. One of my sisters was sent via a taxicab to bring Dr. Aaris back with her. It would take a couple of hours.

Mom, as she cried her heart out, took care of Saleh's wounds. A bullet had grazed him on his left arm. He had been shot on the thigh of his left leg. The bullet wound looked as if some weird creature had dug its way into his thigh. Blood was still flowing from it, but it had slowed down.

By the time Dr. Aaris arrived with my sister, Saleh was losing consciousness. We kept on talking to him in order to keep him from closing his eyes. I tried to help, but every time I looked at my brother Saleh, his sad face and the pain in his eyes made me almost scream out in tears. But in my young mind, I knew that would not be productive.

Dr. Aaris treated the wound, and hooked Saleh up to the IV serum he had brought with him. He shouted questions at Hamayoon while he worked on Saleh. He wanted to know when the last time they had eaten was. What had they eaten? How long ago was he shot? When did the blood flow slow down?

Through tears of his own, Hamayoon answered most of the Doctor's questions. He did all he could, and announced at the end with a tired smile on his face that Saleh is a Monis. Father and Mother smiled at the announcement. They knew that the joke meant Saleh was tough and that he would survive this.

As the days passed and he got better, he finally went into the Kabul Municipal Hospital to get a x-ray and see where the bullet was. He also talked to a surgeon to see if there was a way to remove the bullet. The surgeon informed him that the bullet fragment was lodged between two main arteries in his leg. If they attempted to remove it, there was a chance that they might hit an artery causing him to bleed to death. And the other option, he wondered? The answer was that the bullet fragment would not cause any kind of infections if it stayed where it was. The only discomfort would be that when the weather got a little colder, it would bother him. Also, whenever he went through the surveillance systems, it would set off the alarms. But in light of bleeding to death, this option was much better.

Father moved fast. Within a week after this incident he had found another smuggler. They could leave immediately for Pakistan. Father was trying to get the whole family out now. He had figured out that living in Afghanistan was no longer a good idea. He decided that Hamayoon and Dauod, our two brothers ripe for the draft, as well as my sisters Shakiba and Feriba would all leave in this trip. My eldest sister Sarah and her husband also wanted to leave. They joined this group. They also had two children to carry along with them. The price of being smuggled out at this time had risen from 15,000 to 20,000 Afghani Rupees per head. Child price was 15,000. Father got the money together and within another week, they left Afghanistan.

~ Chapter Three ~

The Perilous Journey

The smuggler who was to carry the members of our family across the border to Pakistan was a heartless bastard. As with all the others of his type, the money had to be given to him prior to the trip. Since the journey would be one where everyone's life was in danger, there was no refund and you traveled at your own risk. If a surprise attack by looters and or other groups occurred, you had to fend for yourself. He would try to survive by helping only himself.

This journey began in Kabul and the group traveled by pickup trucks to the Province of Ningarhar. From Jalalabad, the city in the province of Ningarhar, located southeast of Kabul, they then traveled toward the Khyber Pass, which forms the border between Afghanistan and Pakistan. At this point the journey would become perilous, for the rest of the way would be on foot. They would have to cross the mountains. The group would have three donkeys that would be used for carrying luggage. They had to walk on foot and carry their children with them as well. To avoid any kind of problems and stay inconspicuous, the majority of their journey would take place at night.

The mountain range of Hindu Kush, part of the chain of the Himalayan Mountains runs throughout Afghanistan. The name Hindu Kush translated into English means *killer of Hindus.* So named because of the rough terrain that it offers. The group would have to cross part of this rocky mountain. It is hard enough to climb during daylight; they had to cross at night.

In addition to my sisters, brothers, niece, and nephew, the smuggler had three other families making the journey into Pakistan with him. As they cross the mountains, the need for rest becomes necessary. One of the children is crying as his father carries him. The child is hungry, and there is no food except for the stale bread that has been in the Father's pocket for a couple of days now. He gives a piece of the bread to his son to quiet him as the smuggler warns him, "This journey is fucking tough enough without your child announcing it to the whole world. If he cries again, I'll force you to stay with him around here. We will leave you behind."

The parent looks at his son with moist eyes and tries to explain to him that he must try to be quiet. Another couple is holding their daughter's hand as they climb up the mountain range. The father has to sneeze, so he releases his daughter's hand for a second. Unknowingly, the mother also releases her daughter's hand at this time. The child screams as she tumbles down the mountain.

With horror-stricken faces, both of them rush to her side. She is badly hurt, and needs medical attention. The sad fact is that there is no doctor among them. "Leave her. There's nothing you can do for her anymore," says the smuggler.

With shock on their faces, they look in disbelief at the smuggler.

"We have to be on the other side by dawn. If you want to carry her on your back, and hope that she's still alive by the time we get to the other side you can. Otherwise, leave her here and let's go. You are wasting valuable time."

The parents hold their daughter in their bosoms. They try to console her, and they tell her that everything will be okay, but the look on her face and the horror that she sees in her parents' faces tells another story. The smuggler begins climbing up the mountain once again and tells the group to do the same. They all obediently follow. He shouts to the two, who are still holding their injured daughter, "This is your last chance. Come with us or stay with her. She's dead. There's nothing you can do."

They eventually catch up to the group, having left their alive, but injured child on the doorsteps of death. The couple is silent as silent tears keep flowing down the woman's face.

During many such journeys, thousands of Afghans were killed and looted. Sometimes the smugglers whom these people trusted turned out to be part of the raiders. The Afghans would figure out too late that they had come to the middle of nowhere just to have everything taken away from them. At other times there were blizzards as well that made the journey impossible to complete. Despite all the perils, the chance of freedom from the tyranny that had become Afghanistan made many risk their lives and take a chance.

The journeys that the people made into Pakistan from Afghanistan was through to different entry points. Those, as was the case with me and my family, who lived in the northern and central tier of the country went through the Khyber Pass into Peshawar, Pakistan. The people who lived in the southern or western regions of Afghanistan went through the province of Kandahar into Quetta, Pakistan. I did not know it at that time, but the majority of people who lived in central and northern Afghanistan are mainly of the more moderate Muslim groups that have descended from the Uzbeks, Tajiks, and Turkmen—all of them have some resemblance to the Mongols who had tried to conquer them many years before—I know now why I have small eyes. The people who lived in the South were mainly Pushtuns—the hard-line followers of Islam. Even at this time, there was an ethnic divide in place within Afghanistan.

The members of our family who were making this odyssey were fortunate enough to make it to Pakistan. By the arrival of dawn, an exhausted group of travelers rounded the top of the Hindu Kush. The rest of the trip was downhill and much easier. But getting this far had not been as easy as it seems when it is written on the pages of a book.

The couple who left their daughter behind began to argue about one hour after the incident. Apparently, the man had convinced his wife to leave their daughter behind, and make the rest of the journey. She had agreed initially, but now she was no longer as accepting of what her husband had decided.

She turned to walk back to where she had left her daughter. Her husband tried to stop her. "Let me go," she screamed. "I'd rather die in this wilderness than live without my daughter. She is a piece of me; I can't leave her like that."

He was trying to be an understanding husband as he tried to console his wife, but the smuggler was not. "This is a family affair, and you need to take care of it. It doesn't concern the rest of us, so we will keep going."

He marched right along with the group as he left the couple behind. A few of the travelers looked back a couple of times, but in the end no one knew what happened to the couple. They were left behind.

Late the next morning, the group made it to Peshawar, Pakistan. Peshawar was the stopping ground for many of the Afghans as well as the smuggler. Most of these Afghans would become part of the large group that lived in overcrowded camps along the dry lands of Peshawar. That for many was better than living in the war-torn cities of Afghanistan.

The Monis family still had another fifty or so miles to travel. Their final destination was Islamabad, the capital of Pakistan.

They eventually made it there and started the process of earning a living there while they waited for my eldest brother, Nadir, who was in USA to once again sponsor them as refugees to the US.

~ Chapter Four ~

An Unexpected Hurdle

The troubles of the Monis family had just begun. For the first time in our lives, our close-knit family was separated. I had two brothers in America, one of whom I had never met; three sisters and two brothers in Pakistan; and the rest of us were still in Afghanistan.

Father was planning on moving the whole family out, but as the school year started, and he went back to Mazaar-e-Sharif, the city in the northern province where he worked, things seemed normal for the time.

That fall we felt the aftershocks of what had become our life. That day in the fall of 1987 was a beautiful one. Not a cloud was in the sky, and the temperature rested at 75 degrees. The breeze was blowing ever so slightly. In retrospect, the irony is that the day should have been a dark and gloomy one. I have learned, however, that things in life are not always as they appear.

That afternoon after I had returned from school, not even an hour had passed when the doorbell rang. For some odd reason, of all the members of the family who were present in our household, I was the chosen one to open the door. I still wish I had not.

After about the third ring of the doorbell, I finally opened it. Outside the door stood my aunts and uncles who lived in the north where Father worked. I remember wondering, "Why are they all here?" They rarely visited us in Kabul. When they did, they never all visited at the same time.

The somberness in their faces made me think that something was wrong. When they moved aside, the horror within my heart was confirmed.

They carried with them a wooden box that was about 6' tall and 3' wide. I knew that it contained the dead body of my Father, but I was not ready to accept the reality of this nightmare. My Father had walked out on his own two feet, and I expected him to return that way as well. As usual in the Afghan tradition that we had come to expect, the details of how Father died were sketchy. A heart attack was said to be the cause of death, but there was no one in the immediate family in Mazar at the time of his death to confirm what really happened to him.

They entered the house and took the coffin into the guestroom. The unpleasant sounds of crying that reverberated through the house, as our family learned about Father's demise was horrible.

I still was not ready to accept the fact. I remember thinking that this is not real. I walked around the yard a few times. In my young mind, the concept of death was not that concrete. I was not ready to accept death as part of life.

I finally worked up the nerve to go into the guestroom and view Father's coffin. They had removed the cover so that his face could show. The whole experience was surreal. I didn't know how to feel as I walked up to the coffin. I had not cried until that moment, but upon looking at Father's blue, pale, emotionless face, I burst out in tears. Even now, I can't explain why people cry upon seeing a dead person's face, but at that moment I cried like a little baby. I guess it might be because of all the overwhelming emotions that we cannot express in any other way except by tears. Whatever the reason, I cried like I never have before or since. The face that I saw that day will forever be engraved in my mind.

About a month after the funeral, my older brother, Saleh, took charge of the Monis family. He thought it might be a good idea for all of us to see the place of Father's work. So for the first time, I got to travel by bus to another province of the country. The trip was a good one for me for it gave me a glimpse of the hard work Father had done to get the Monis family to where we were. I realized that Father used the same vigor and drive in his work as he did on Friday nights when he partied with his friends.

We spent about a month in the province of Balkh in the city of Mazaar-e-Sharif. When the vacation was over, we had to travel back to Kabul, but Saleh had to stay there in order to run the factory. Uncle Nasir wanted to go to Kabul for a visit, so he volunteered to go with us. Little did I know that morning when I stepped into the bus that was set to go to Kabul that my life was about to take another turn for the worst.

I have a habit of napping during long trips. Given the rough, unpaved roads we were traveling, this trip was one of about five hours. Anyway, I took a nap in the bus that morning, and either because I sleepwalked, something I don't do that often; or because I had amnesia, more plausible, I don't remember the events I am about to retell. This is the story I was told when I woke up in the Kabul Municipal Hospital.

Our bus broke down that morning about an hour into the trip. The bus pulled to the side of the road for repair. I exited the bus telling Mom that I needed to get a breath of fresh air. Mom assumed that I would get off the bus and not venture across the street. That is exactly what I did. I tried to cross the street. Since our bus was blocking the view of oncoming busses, as I stepped into the street, a bus traveling at speeds of over sixty miles per hour hit me. I flew about fifty yards. Upon hitting the side of the road, I lay there unconscious. My left femur, the strongest bone in the human body, was broken; my left knee was banged up; my hands were bleeding. I guess I must have presented a terrifying sight. The bus that had hit me was the bus that transported me along with my family to the hospital.

Uncle Nasir was the male who was traveling with Mom, my sister Roya, and me. Knowing the cultural gossip and rumors that would be spread about him—most people would say that he was responsible for my getting hurt because he did not pay enough attention—he must have felt pretty bad. He was upset too obviously because when I landed in the hospital, the doctors only informed him that I was in a deep coma and there was the possibility that I might not make it. Mom tells me that Uncle Nasir looked worried, but when asked how I would be he would say, "He'll be fine."

I spent three weeks in a coma. During that time, the doctors did not put a cast on my broken femur to start its healing process. Given the lack of resources that the hospital had, were I to die, the plaster cast would be wasted. Although I see their point, it still bothers me that they did that. Bastards!

Obviously I lived. I spent three months at home in a cast. The plaster cast ran from the tip of my toe up to my waist. I was bedridden. Mom, bless her heart, served as my caretaker during this time.

Saleh as the head of the family was as hard at work in continuing what Father had started as Father himself would have been were he still alive. He had found a smuggler who charged the highest price of any smugglers we had dealt with prior. He also promised things that many smugglers could not even dream about.

His name was Taj Mohammed. He was about 5' 9" in height, and he had long, flowing, jet-black hair as well as facial hair of the same brilliant color. He had deep, penetrating eyes, but the most striking feature about him was that he only had one leg. He claimed that on one of his trips he had stepped on a land mine that had blown off his left leg. He volunteered to show off his scars from the accident, but everyone believed his story, and we all declined.

Taj Mohammed was able to offer a lot of security to his customers because he could not walk. After he had his leg blown off, he had to find an alternate way of smuggling people or find a new career. He did the former. He charged 35,000 Afghani Rupees per head. For this money, he promised that nothing would happen to the livelihood of the persons who made the trek across with him. He also promised that he would personally escort every one of his customers to the exact destination that they wanted to go.

Saleh as well as the rest of us were impressed with his credentials. We hired him to smuggle my sister Roya, Mom, and me out of the country. Saleh had decided that he would stay in Afghanistan along with his wife and three kids and run the factory. He felt that he was not in danger. He promised that when he saw things turn worse, he would leave the country.

Everything was set up so that as soon as I finished my physical therapy—my leg would not bend at the knee since it had been straight in a cast for three months—we would leave the country. In the fall of 1987, the time finally came. Taj Mohammed smuggled us out of Afghanistan.

~ Chapter Five ~

A Step toward Paradise

That morning when we left Afghanistan, Taj showed up at about five in the morning to pick us up. My sister, Roya, and I had stayed up late the previous night playing with my cousins who had come over as well as my nieces and nephews who lived with us.

I remember that when Mom tried to wake me, I wanted to sleep more, but I knew the time had come to leave Afghanistan. Thinking back to those days, the fact that I never even got to say bye to all my friends from school was kind of sad. Most of them never talked about leaving Afghanistan. I wonder if any of them did. I also wonder how many of them are still alive. The fragility of life illuminates itself in this manner every time I think about all the things that have happened to this family and its friends as we have all lived this life.

The Taxi cab was waiting outside the house, and after about twenty minutes from the time I was awakened, we left the house in which I was born forever. As I climbed into the backseat of the cab, and as it began its journey toward the bus station, I took a long last look at the house—the two story white house in the Guzargah neighborhood is forever etched in the realm of my memories. I kept looking at it until it became smaller and smaller and then disappeared from my view. I faced forward in my seat finally, and there was an uneasy silence in the cab. Taj was sitting in front, Mom, Roya, and I were in the back. The radio played an Afghan song about love. Thinking back, I assume that Mom and Roya probably had the same jubilant yet scared feeling that I had, but none of us said anything. Our journey out of Afghanistan had just begun. There were many obstacles that awaited us.

As we traveled in the cab, the morning was trying to end the reign of night. The first rays of sunshine were peeking through the Hindu Kush Mountains. The day was going to be a beautiful one.

We got into the bus circle about thirty minutes later. There was a lot of hustle and bustle of the morning travelers. Most of these travelers were going to the city of Jalalabad in the province of Ningarhar. Some of the other occupants of the bus may also have been escaping Afghanistan, but no one mentioned anything about it. Even on these busses, there were governmental spies who tried to stop people from leaving the country. That was the reason no one trusted anyone else. For this same reason, most people distrusted one another. I couldn't believe that the country I loved was turning into this!

The bus was set to leave at eight o'clock sharp. One of the more able men that were traveling with us began unloading the taxicab that we had arrived in. There was a lot of luggage between all of the families that were traveling. Like a greyhound, this bus had a luggage compartment at the side. The luggage was somewhat mistreated as the men tossed them into the bus. We boarded the bus a little after the entire luggage had been loaded. The families that were traveling all had a somber smile on their faces. It was bittersweet to leave Kabul, which for most of us was the place of our births.

The bus ride was long and boring. I wanted to doze off because I had not had enough sleep the previous night, but for fear of getting into another accident like the last time I had napped on a bus, I did not let myself fall asleep. About eleven o'clock that morning we stopped at a roadside teahouse. They had different pastries as well as both green and black teas. The travelers all descended the bus and had a bite to eat or got something to drink. I had a cup of tea—black with no sugar or milk. Roya and Mom had the same. Roya had a pastry as well. Taj Mohammed paid for all of the people. I guess it was his way of compensating for the outrageous amount he had charged everyone. By midday the bus was back on the road. We got into Jalalabad about three o'clock that afternoon.

At that point we discovered that Taj was meeting another family in Jalalabad. They had not arrived yet. He said that he had to wait for them to arrive before we could all leave for Pakistan. He got all of the families cabs, and we went to the nearest motel in Jalalabad. We were told that we would have to stay the night in this city. Tomorrow would be the day we would leave for Pakistan.

The so-called motel was nothing but a dingy room. No furnishing of any kind was present with the exception of three straw cots and three cloth sheets. There were no pillows in sight anywhere. I guess this was the way we would sleep tonight. Taj was in the adjacent motel room as he came and informed us of his whereabouts. He also said that if we needed anything, we should not hesitate to call on him. I presume all the other families received the same information.

The next morning, we were delighted at the news that the other family who was to travel with us had now arrived. We would all go to one of Taj's friend's house first. Then, we would set off toward the Khyber Pass.

We traveled to his friend's house. They were quite hospitable given the large number of us. His friend's family provided everyone with tea as well as lunch. As we were ready to leave, the reason for the visit here became apparent.

Taj's friend brought a waxy, brown substance, and handed it to Taj.

"Is this the exact weight we talked about?" asked Taj.

His friend shook his head, "Yes."

Taj examined the pure opium as I found out later, and asked for an iron. To me the opium looked like play dough, although the color was kind of weird.

After the iron had become warm enough to melt the opium, Taj flattened it into rectangular pieces that measured to about three inches in length, and seven inches in width. Just as I was wondering what he would do with it, he asked me to come to him.

I looked at Mom with surprise, and seeing that she had no objections, I obeyed.

He fitted the rectangles at the soles of my feet, and then told me to put on my socks followed by my shoes on top of them. I obeyed.

I walked a few steps inside the house after I had put my shoes on. "They are not bothersome, are they?" asked Taj.

I said, "No," I hated the fact that I had been the lucky one that he chose to smuggle his drugs for him. I guess he figured that since I was young, no one would suspect me.

He said, "Good."

He began gathering his stuff, and we were finally on our way to Pakistan.

The majority of our trip toward the border took place in two pickup trucks. I think they were Toyotas. On the ledges of the bed of the truck, boards had been nailed as makeshift seats. There was a brown tarpaulin that served as the camper for these two pickups. The luggage was tossed into the center of the truck bed. Around the board seats the women sat holding their children on their laps. Some of the children were seated on top of the luggage. All the families fit into the two trucks. The trip was kind of boring. The barren, war-torn Jalalabad was beautiful in an antique way. Most of the charred trees still lay there in the somberness of the afternoon. The guards who manned the checkpoints along the way almost looked as lifeless as those trees. They took their jobs seriously enough, but the tediousness probably had gotten to them.

Our pickups were pulled over twice for search and questioning prior to getting to the border. The men wanted to know what the nature of our travel was. Taj did most of the talking. One of the other men who aided him in his endeavor also did some of the talking. All of us were asked to stay put inside unless asked by the guards to come out.

It was on the second round of stops that I saw how seriously these guards took their jobs. As our trucks were pulled to the side of the road for inspection, a car going at a high speed tried to dodge the checkpoint. All the guards present at the scene—four of them—took their AK-47 Rifles off their shoulders and began shooting at the car. It veered off the road, and hit a tree. Bullets had made the body of the car look like a snowflake. After the car had come to a stop, they resumed their inspection of the trucks as if nothing out of the ordinary had happened.

In my young mind, this seemed horrible. I wanted to jump out, and go see if the people inside the car were okay. I looked at Mom. As if having some kind of telepathic power, she gave me the look that said, "Stay where you are. This is not your business. Don't make it your business."

Shrugging my shoulders at her, and shifting my gaze away from her eyes, I began imagining how cool it would be to cross the border. I had heard stories about Khyber Pass. Father was big on history. He had told me a story about the Pass, and how it was considered the passageway between the East and the West. He had also talked about Genghis Khan and his Mongol Hordes. How they traveled through the Pass as part of their Silk Road.

Without much trouble, we got through this checkpoint. Of all the travelers, I was probably the most dangerous. I was carrying drugs into Pakistan with me, a no-no. Well, we finally got to the Khyber Pass. I had envisioned it to be a big, elaborate place, but it was not. It was a chain that served as the demarcation line between two sovereign nations. Taj Mohammed produced a piece of document that had the official seal of the government of Afghanistan to the border guards. They eyed the document nonchalantly, and then began calling out the names that had been printed on the document. They checked each one of our identification cards as well to make sure that the names matched the faces. They did.

Taj Mohammed's scheme had now become clear to me. He used some of the money that he charged people as kickback to get these types of forged documents from the governmental officials. Not a bad plan. I have learned that money can get you anything you want, I guess Afghanistan was no exception to this rule.

After they had checked all of us, the document was given back to Taj. The guard gave the okay sign to the chain-guard and he unhooked the chain. The border had been opened for us to pass through. We all passed through. Although I did not give it much thought at the time it happened. Now as I think back, I am kind of awestruck at the fact that for a split second as I was crossing through the Khyber Pass, I had a foot in each country. For a split second, I stood in both Pakistan and Afghanistan. That is something that few in the world experience.

~ Chapter Six ~

The New Land

We had now entered the border town of Peshawar, Pakistan. Although the major language of Pakistan is Urdu, the majority of the people who live in this town are the descendants of the Pashtun Tribes. They used to be tough warriors who fought back in the time of the British Occupation. They were the ones who lent a hand in driving the British out of this area. Even today, most Hindi people are afraid of the Pashtuns, whom they call the Pathans.

The Pushtuns that live in the Peshawar area speak Pushtu, which is the other major language in Afghanistan besides Dari Persian. I heard a little bit of Urdu around this area, but the driver who awaited us on this side of the border was a Pushtun. He and Taj spoke for a minute. We all got into the same type of pickup in which we had ridden up to the Khyber Pass on the other side. The trip in this truck would end when we got into the center of the city.

Unlike the previous time, this time I took a seat right by the edge of the truck, where I would have a clearer view of the outside. To my disappointment there was not much there to see. The mountainous terrain that we traveled on was rough and bumpy. There was just enough room for the truck to pass through the narrow road at the edge of the mountain. There were no guardrails. If the driver maneuvered incorrectly, we would all tumble down the side of this rocky mountain and plunge to our deaths. The barrenness of the land and the grayish rockiness of the mountains were appealing to a degree as well since I had never before paid this much attention to either.

As we made our trip into town, evening was fast approaching. We got into town in about forty-five minutes. By now only one other family remained in the truck besides us. They were next on the drop off list. They were going to their relatives' house that had obviously convinced them to leave Afghanistan.

When we got there, the family that came out of the house to greet their guests was overwhelmingly ecstatic. They kissed Taj Mohammed's hands as if he were some kind of king or something. At that moment it dawned on me that to many people he was like a savior. He was their last hope of leaving the shit that had become their lives behind.

The family asked us to come in for tea and something to eat. They said, "You all are probably weary from the journey. Tea will relax you." They also said that although they were now in a foreign land, they had not and would not forget the Afghan hospitality. Taj accepted and we all went to have tea and something to eat. When we were in the house, I had to use the restroom. Taj was waiting outside the bathroom as I came out of it. He said, "Go back into the bathroom, and give me the stuff you are carrying for me."

I went back into the bathroom. I took my socks off and removed the rectangular pieces of opium. I had already taken my shoes off upon entering the house—a cultural thing that shows a sign of respect. I handed him the opium, and he placed it into the pocket of his woolen coat he had on over his traditional Afghan garb called *Perahan Tumban*.

Since our truck driver had left after he dropped us off at this house, we had to get a cab now in order to travel to our final destination. Islamabad is the capital of Pakistan and is located southwest of Peshawar. The distance between the two cities is about 60 miles. Given the rough conditions of the roads, however, the trip takes about an hour and a half.

When the cab arrived in front of the apartment complex in Islamabad, it was already dark. The cities in Pakistan were not that different from those I had lived in in Afghanistan. The lights in the stores illuminated the streets about halfway. Taj Mohammed, as he had promised, made the trip all the way here with us.

I got off the cab; Mom told me that my brother-in-law, Sarah's husband, Nabi, who had made the trip with the others, should be in front of the store. He had a French fry vending machine just like those pretzel sellers in cities here. There was a bunch of people gathered around him. They all wanted some fries. To suit the Pakistani taste, Nabi had created a mix of spices that would make the fries a little spicy. I guess he had done well from the way he was doing business.

I went up to him, and tapped him on the arm. He thought I was a customer and said a few words in Urdu that I did not understand. So I said his name and started speaking Dari to him.

He looked down at me, and began smiling widely. "Hey, how are you?" he said.

"Exhausted. It has been a long trip," I have always prided myself on being direct.

He bent down to give me a hug, and picked me up in his arms as if I were a child. Well, I guess I was a child—only eleven years old.

He told his customers that he'd be right back. The shop owner in front of whose shop was his little vending machine was told to keep an eye on his stuff. He set me down, and started running. He was out of sight. I walked back to the cab confused, and said, "Nabi ran up the stairs after I said 'hi' to him."

Within minutes, Nabi returned along with both of my brothers. They thanked Taj, and invited him to come upstairs for tea. He declined saying that he had family in this town to visit.

They unloaded the luggage from the trunk and we all went upstairs into the apartments that they called home.

Sarah, Nabi, and her two kids occupied one of the apartments on the third floor. My brothers Dauod, Hamayoon, and my sisters Shakiba, and Feriba occupied the apartment across from them. They had lived here a little more than a year now. The shop owner in front of whose store Nabi had his fries vending was also the owner of this complex.

It was nice in a way to be reunited with them. Immediately the stove was fired up so that they could make food and tea for us. Nabi brought some fresh fries from downstairs. He then excused himself saying, "I'll be up as soon as I close down downstairs."

This was Pakistan. We had made it. I wondered how long we would live here. I also wondered how soon I would learn this language. All of those questions would be answered in a matter of time.

~ Chapter Seven ~

Revelations

As we had tea and relaxed in this new land in which we had arrived a short while ago, the conversations were plentiful. Everyone wanted to talk about the past, and how we had all escaped, and how we had all faced perils as well along the way.

As the evening wore on, the topic of our discussions became more and more interesting. New revelations were illustrated about the Monis family that I had not heard before. I don't know the exact reasons as to why all these facts had been kept secret from me. It may have been either that they thought I was too young or that telling me might have jeopardized the family's well being.

Although we thought that Father was opposed to the regime that had replaced the king in Afghanistan, he never showed any preference one way or the other. He supported every family member's decision to do what he or she wanted. When Saleh wanted to join the Afghan army and fight against the rebels, Father gave him his support. When Dauod decided to join the organization Afghan Students against Communism through the university, Father nodded his support. Even when the female members of the Monis family decided to join some type of coalition, again Father gave his support. For example, Homaira, my widowed sister whose husband passed away in

1985, who lived with us, decided that she was going to join the *Hizb*—a word that means coalition, Father supported her.

Homaira's background story is kind of interesting, and needs to be told at this point in this story. Although she and her three kids were one of the last groups of the Monises to leave Afghanistan, she had gone through a lot in Afghanistan as a result of the Communist Regime. Her husband, Latif, was a worker at the Afghan Airport, Aryana, as a meteorologist. There was a crackdown within the airport. Some of the workers were suspected of espionage. Therefore, the whole airport was under scrutiny. Latif, just like the majority of the Monis family, was an avid adversary of the Russian-backed Communist government that had taken over the country. Since he had access to more information firsthand, he was approached more than once by groups who wanted to print classified information in their leaflets—something I'll talk about a lot more in a little bit.

Anyway, on a sunny spring afternoon, Latif left work on his way home. He rode the bus to and from work. It was about 5:00 in the evening. My sister, Homaira, and her husband were one of the few people in the Monis family who had a phone line. On this particular day, Latif's boss phoned my sister about six times in the time span between the hours of five and eight in the evening. His final call came at eight—three hours after Latif had left work. My sister was told that her husband had had a heart attack on the bus, and she needed to go to the hospital to see him. Latif was pronounced dead in the hospital before his wife, and his relatives made it there.

We, the Monis family including my sister Homaira, wanted the doctors to do an autopsy to find out the exact cause of death. He was only in his twenties. He did not smoke or drink and his family history did not include a prevalence of heart attacks. That is why we were all convinced that his death might have been caused by something else. However, his mother said that she did not want her son torn to bits. He had suffered enough as far as she was concerned. If men were responsible for his death, and not God, God would punish all that were guilty. She said that she wanted to put her faith in God, and leave it at that. We let her have her wish—she was a grieving mother after all. But according to us, the real reason Latif died was because the government got rid of him. He was a threat to them because he was an intelligent and charismatic man who had the potential of leading those that were against the Russian-backed Communist government in a revolt.

Getting back to Father and his support for all of us, he even supported the younger members of the Monis family as they chose sides and explored the different groups that were available. When Hamayoon would do things like distribute leaflets, which I mentioned earlier, he did not object. The leaflets were called *Shabnameh* or night letters—named so because they were distributed at night. They would be thrown into residents' yards. A knock would follow this action so that the people could come and get the letters. These leaflets normally had essays, and news articles written that showed the faults of the government. The Afghan people, one article claimed, had the right to know what kinds of atrocities this Communist government was committing.

There were only a certain number of the families that received these leaflets. The residential houses, into which these leaflets were thrown, were somehow identified as anti-government. One way to let the group know that you were in support of them was to light a flare firecracker, and let it go off at 10:00 PM. Hamayoon used to do this also. He got in trouble once over doing this, but Father was not angry over the fact that Hamayoon was doing it; he was angry over the fact that Hamayoon was not doing it correctly.

I used to watch my brother as he prepped the flare. It was kind of exciting watching him put so much effort and meticulous planning into something that only lasted seconds.

On one particular night, Hamayoon went through his usual routine of preparing the flare. As he shot it off, Father came out of the house. He asked Hamayoon, "What the hell are you doing?"

"What I usually do. I am shooting a flare."

"Do you know what time it is?" asked Father.

"Ugh, it's 9:20," said my brother.

"I thought so," said Father, "If you are gonna do this, then do it right. The time to shoot off flares is designated as ten o'clock."

"So what if it is forty minutes early," protested Hamayoon.

"It's pointless if it is early. You just wasted all that time as well as a good-looking flare. Next time pay more attention to the time." Father retreated back into the house. Hamayoon started preparing a second flare to shoot off exactly at ten.

Father also supported me when I wanted to join a Boy-Scouts-type group through school. The group was called Students are the Future. It was a leadership building organization. The purpose of it was to make us loyal to the government so that our generation would continue the regime to its pinnacle. Although not a well-run organization, it did garner me a few good friends, and I learned to be a louder person. I used to be the shy kid who kept to himself before that.

Because of all the activities that the various members of our family were involved in, our house would be searched more often than that of our neighbors. Although Afghanistan had now become a communist nation, in the years of the Shah, or the king, there was a constitution that had been drawn up. One of its provisions mentioned frequent search and seizure as a nuisance. There had to be due cause, and an official okay had to be given before any searches could occur. This new government totally ignored the constitution; they did whatever their hearts pleased.

I learned that night as we sat in the apartment in Pakistan and sipped tea that the main reason Father had wanted us to leave Afghanistan was not just the fact that the family had members who were of the draft age. I learned that we were an active family, the majority of whose members were involved in some kind of anti-government organization. I also learned that night that even those members of the family who had joined pro-government groups still harbored feelings against the government. Maybe Father knew this all along, and that is why he supported all of us so willingly. Maybe he also knew that we would all find our way by helping one another after he was gone. He was a brilliant man who had a grand plan that is being engraved only now as I think back on all these things.

~ Chapter Eight ~

The Routine in Pakistan

When I approached my brother-in-law's fries vending area that night as we arrived in Islamabad, I assumed that my brothers also did the same thing that Nabi was doing. I found out that the way they were earning a living was different than that which Nabi had chosen. Hamayoon and Dauod had a little shack across from where Nabi had his business. My brothers claimed that they themselves had built the shack. It looked well built. I guess that when necessity arises, men can achieve pretty much whatever task is asked of them.

Within this shack existed a little shop that had rows and files made from wooden blocks. Dauod awoke every morning at five and went to the farmer's market. There he would buy one day's worth of different types of vegetables that we would then sell through the shack. Hamayoon normally woke up at nine. He would at that time go downstairs and open shop. Dauod would arrive at around the same time. After helping Hamayoon with the unloading of all the vegetable arrangements, he would come back into the apartment for breakfast, and sometimes some more sleep. Hamayoon and Dauod worked in this way seven days a week. They divided the nine hours during which the store was open. Normally Hamayoon worked a few extra hours since Dauod was the one who normally did the shopping in the market.

My sisters—Sarah, Shakiba, Feriba, and now Roya were all homebound. None of them went to school. Of them, Shakiba was the age of a high school senior; Feriba was the age of a 9th grader; Roya could have been a 7th grader; and I should have been in 6th grade—that was the year I was in the midst of studying in Afghanistan before all of this had started. Sarah was a high school teacher in Afghanistan. She used to teach Dari, but now she had become a housewife.

They were not total prisoners as are women in some of today's Muslim societies. My sisters and Mom would go to the Bazaars every once in a while. Also, the roof, which was a verandah as well, provided a good view of the streets and the goings-on therein. They also took walks some evenings around the neighborhood.

I was lucky. I was able to go to school in Pakistan. My brother Dauod took me to the school, which my niece and nephew also attended. It was called Daisy-Land Public School. As deceiving as that name may sound, this was a private school. You had to pay to attend, but since it was near where we lived, my brother must have thought highly enough of it. I was signed up at this school after I had been in Pakistan about a week. Since I did not know Urdu, the official language of Pakistan, I was put in the third grade. The school's principal, who was also the owner of the school, thought that was an ideal decision. Neither my brother nor I argued against his recommendation.

I started the third grade that week. Most of the material was easy. I found out that they used the same ranking system, and the top student got an armband-captain-style symbol that Afghan schools had used. Within a month I had enough command of the Urdu language to excel to the first position among these students—I was the one who wore that armband. There was some resentment among some of the Pakistani students since a foreigner had come and stolen the top rank from them so quickly, but the majority of the kids were okay with me. I garnered a few friends quickly.

These guys accepted me into their circle of friendship, and I was invited to their houses to read comic books—a fad that the kids had grabbed onto that year. I was also introduced to the game of cricket, a national past time in Pakistan. I did okay for myself.

School was the top priority since my brother was paying for it. Everyday, I was expected to do my homework before I was allowed to do anything else. Just like Father, Dauod was as vehement about grades. In addition to homework, I was given the chore of manning the store for an hour each day. At the beginning, I did this for fun. As time passed though, I had regrets about working in the store. I would rather have played.

But the fact that I was expected to do the things that I did, helped me build my character. Now that I look back on it, I am glad I was given the responsibilities that I had.

As I have pointed out through the tale of Pakistan so far, it was not all fun and games. As the new kid, I did have to prove myself on the first day of school. Especially when the kids found out that I was partially Pashtun, they immediately assumed that I should be strong and powerful. They wanted to see a showdown. There was a Pakistani Pashtun already in that school. He was the apparent bully of the school, and I was about to face him.

~ Chapter Nine ~

The Battle of the Warriors

His name was Azhar Khan, and he was the one that I was chosen to fight. He was not really a bad guy as I found out later, but at this time we had to fight each other because reputations were at stake. He was a Khan after all. That last name showed a sign of prestige within the Pashtun tribes. The Khans were normally rich and had positions of power within the tribal government.

I did not really want to fight him, but there was no other option for me; I was new to the school and therefore I had to prove myself. I did have an advantage over this guy in that I was a year older at eleven years than he was, but he was a big guy. We were about the same height, but he was darker than I was. He looked more Pashtun than I did. That is one thing about me, I am white—I look white. I get that from my father, although a Pashtun by background, he looked totally white—he even had blond hair and blue eyes.

That morning before class, his thugs tried to get a rise out of me. They pushed me as I walked into our classroom. I was not going to fight this early in the morning though. I let it go, and acted like it did not bother me that they had pushed me. Some of my newly acquired friends in that class though responded by shoving a few of them. The battle lines were being drawn.

At lunchtime, we squared off. Azhar took the first shot, and he landed a good right hook in my lower jaw. I rubbed my jaw, and took my first shot. I hit him in the chin. I had underestimated him, he truly was a Pashtun, and he could fight. We exchanged shots evenly until the principal came and broke us up. He took both of us into his office. The principal was furious. He shouted loudly, and his mouth opened wider than I had ever witnessed any human being's mouth open. As spittle started spewing from the corners of his mouth, he screamed, "What the fuck are you guys doing?"

I guess that owning the school gave him the right to use that kind of language. Neither Azhar nor I said anything. The principal shouted at us a little while longer, and finally he made us shake hands and go back to class.

As we walked to class, I said to Azhar, "I did not really want to fight you today."

"Then why did you?" he demanded.

"To prove myself."

"Well, whatever. You want to pull that shit again, bring it on."

"Listen," I said, "I don't want to fight. I don't want us to get off on the wrong foot. I want to call a truce."

He finally understood what I was trying to tell him. He looked at me with that sense of knowing what he had always known. It is not easy being the feared one in school as he had always been. He knew now that he had a friend who would not be afraid of him, and treat him as a friend not due to fear, but due to understanding. He shook my hand again, and this time the handshake meant that we were going to be the kings of school, but we would not get in each other's way.

Azhar and I got along well from that day on. We even played on the same team in physical education when there were team sports such as cricket or soccer. Granted we were not best friends, but we had an understanding that commanded respect from all of the kids in that school.

~ Chapter 10 ~

Family Conflicts

It is kind of funny looking back at not only the triumphs of the Monis family, but the tribulations as well. As I look back on our conflicts as a family, I realize that we have been no different than any other family that might inhabit the far reaches of the world. The theme of struggle is a universal one. I suppose it is what makes life unique. Imagine a life with no strife; can you do it? Struggle in the domain of life is what makes us unique as individuals. It is the patent of a family's perseverance through the pain that makes that family a marvel for others.

All that I have mentioned before this about struggle has been on the grand scale, but now I want to focus on my family's daily life. Our daily struggle was not that grand, but nonetheless everyday offered its shares of grief.

They say that money is not everything, but as I re-examine my life through the process of writing this book, I realize that even though money may not be everything, it is at the center of most of the things that we want to achieve.

My brothers worked hard at that vegetable store, and for the most part money was plentiful. However, the Monis family had just grown by three. Whereas in the two years that Dauod, Hamayoon, Shakiba, and Feriba had lived in Pakistan, they had figured out how to spend wisely. But now Mom, Roya, and I had been added to the equation. That complicated matters some.

Dauod and Hamayoon never complained about us not having enough money, but on days that business was slow, you could see the strain on their faces.

I knew about the money problem, but there was not much I could do. I wanted to help though, and when I got my allowance for the week on Saturday, the first day of the week since Friday was the only day we were off from school, I invested my allowance in gift wrapping paper, bamboo sticks, and thread. I was about to reopen the business that had garnered me some good cash back in Afghanistan. I spent the next week making kites of different colors, shapes, and sizes. My kite-selling venture went well, and I declined the allowance the next Saturday in order to help out, but Dauod took that as a sign that I did not think his money was good enough for me.

A little word on the men of the Monis family including myself, we all have a rough and rugged exterior, but most of us are sensitive on the inside. Some of us are at times too sensitive. And in the tradition of doing the more sensitive thing, in the end, I took the allowance anyway to keep my brother happy. The thing about money is that if you have too much, you still don't have enough; and when you have too little, the problems arise that you can not solve. In the final analysis though, worrying about money seems to be the central problem that faces most people, and not the actual money itself.

The other conflicts that arose were also rooted in money. Like the argument that escalated into a fist-fight between Dauod and Hamayoon. Hamayoon had a habit of playing video games at the arcade that was located in the vicinity of our apartment. Sometimes, he would be gone for hours. On one particular day, after I had finished my homework, I went downstairs to give Dauod a break from the store. As I sat there surrounded by the vegetables, Dauod seemed a bit more agitated than usual.

"What is the matter?" I asked.

"Your brother," he answered. "He spends all his time and money in those arcades."

With that he left me to man the store as he took off to search for Hamayoon. I used to go with Hamayoon to the arcades every once in a while. There was a cool World Cup Soccer game that we used to play against each other. I also used to face off against him in Fooseball. Anyway, within minutes I saw Hamayoon coming out of the arcades followed by Dauod. Neither of them looked happy, and as they approached the store and went toward the apartment, I could hear them arguing.

Once they got inside the apartment is when the argument turned more heated. Dauod as the older brother was trying to give advice to Hamayoon over what he should and should not do, but Hamayoon being angry was not hearing even one word that Dauod said.

"I am old enough to decide what to do and how to do it. Get off my back."

"Look, Hamayoon, you can't spend all your time in those places. You waste the money that we can use for other things," said Dauod.

"Oh, is that what this is about, money? If that is the case, I'll work in another place and spend the money I earn there in the arcades."

"That was not what I meant," said Dauod, but it was too late.

"What the hell do you want from me, I work like seven hours a day. I deserve some time for fun as well."

"Balance the two."

"Balance, fuck the balance," said Hamayoon.

Dauod like the rest of the Monis family was raised by strict military guidelines that Father had set. One of those guidelines included no profanity toward people who were older than you. Obviously Hamayoon's use of the *F* word got the better of Dauod's nerves. He struck first.

They hit each other as they vented the frustration that had built up inside both of them. The Monis women tried to stop the fighting. Mom, Shakiba, Feriba, and Roya were all at home at that moment. Nabi, the only male nearby was in his apartment peeling potatoes for the evening. Nabi came over to our apartment and broke them apart with the help of my sisters and Mom.

Before being broken apart though, the two of them had gotten off some good shots at each other. Dauod had one disadvantage in this fight. He wore glasses. Without the glasses, his eyesight is not much better than that of a blind person. Within the first few shots, Dauod's glasses broke and fell off thus giving Hamayoon the opportunity to land more punches.

When Dauod came downstairs about an hour and a half later to relieve me from duty at the store, his glasses were taped together because of the fight. He also had a reddened cheek from the blows. Although I wanted to ask him what happened, I knew better than to ask him about it at that moment.

When I got upstairs, Hamayoon was not in the apartment. I knew that he had gone back to the arcades; that was his sanctuary from the realities of life—his escape. Within a day my brothers were speaking to each other again and no mention was made of their fight. Although no one thought about or directly tackled it head on, the main reason for their quarrel was money. But the fact that remains is despite all of the conflicts that we faced the family's tight nit in the end worked to strengthen all of us. I presume that may be the reason the saying, "Money isn't everything," is often uttered. It is because of money that problems arise, although a problem can be tackled well when a family-structure full of strength is in place.

~ Chapter Eleven ~

The Interview

After having lived for about a year in Pakistan, the day finally arrived in the spring of 1988 when we got word that we were on the list of interviewees the U.S. government was considering for asylum into the U.S. This was exciting news since the latter members of the Monis family—Dauod, Hamayoon, Shakiba, and Feriba had waited three years already. There was a glimmer of bad news as well with this development. Mom could not go with us because she had to be summoned via a visa invitation. I still can't figure out why this was one of the rules, but according to INS (Immigration and Naturalization Services) that was the policy. Also since Sarah was married, my brother Nadir, who served as sponsor for all the rest of us, could not summon her. She and her family had to wait until Mom got to the U.S. Mom would be able to sponsor them. All this still seems like a bunch of red tape as I write about it now, but I have learned in the years of my life spent in this great United States that red tape is as much a part of life as is the desire we all have for freedom and peace of mind.

The actual wait before we got word from the American Embassy in Pakistan for the interview was unbearable. We waited about three months from the time that word arrived, which announced that we were on the list, to the time when we were actually told when the interview would be. Finally, in August of 1988 we went to the American Embassy for the interview.

The American government sent an INS representative every year to interview potential candidates who would be eligible for asylum into the U.S. The letter that they sent to us made this guy seem like the most important person we would ever come in contact with. In a way, he was very important because he did hold the fate of the Monis family in his hands. His signature on the document—depending on which side the signature would be located—meant going to the U.S.A or staying forever in Pakistan.

On the day of the interview, we all dressed up in our best clothes. Dauod had been told that dressing up helped your chances of getting accepted. We were not taking any chances. We had to get a large cab to fit all of us, and the cab ride was kind of nerve-wracking. Everyone seemed to be fidgety. I guess this was a big deal, but at the time I was old enough to know and young enough not to get bogged down with its implications the way adults normally do.

When the cab finally stopped in front of the American Embassy in downtown Islamabad, I was surprised to see people waiting by the door. In the tradition of all bureaucratic institutions in Pakistan, this was no exception to the rule. The place was in disarray mainly because the system that the Pakistanis had figured out for interviewing people was messed up. All the families who had been summoned on that day were expected to wait outside the barred gates of the embassy. Every hour a short, stout Pakistani man with a wad of printed names in hand would come out and call the surname of the family that was to go next. Then the gate opened far enough to let the members of that family in. It was totally disorganized. Also in the tradition of the cultural norms of the country, people whose names were not called tried to shove their way through the gate as well. I don't know why they did this because if their name had not been called, there was no interview for them as of yet. I guess being inside of the gates made them feel better. No matter how much they tried pushing their way inside, they never succeeded.

The wait for us came to an end after about an hour when the bald-headed, short man came to the gate and called our name. Through the small opening of the steel gate, all of the members of the Monis family crept inside the embassy. The man led us into the embassy. It was nice looking inside. It looked so immaculate that I thought I had already arrived in the paradise I had so long dreamed of. We were led down the corridor into a small room where there was a long rectangular table surrounded by plush office-type chairs. The man who had led us here informed us that we were to sit here and wait for the American Agent. Dauod asked, "How long will it be before he shows up?"

"A few minutes. He is finishing up paper work on the previous family he interviewed."

"Does he speak Urdu?" asked my brother.

"No. He will have a Pakistani interpreter who will interpret his questions for you, and then interpret your answers to him."

With that the man left all six of us in the room by ourselves. Dauod, since he was the oldest male and thus the leader among us, said that he was going to answer all the questions, but one of my sisters pointed out that it would look bad if the INS Agent asked the questions from someone else and

Dauod answered. We decided that Dauod would take the general questions where no one in particular would be addressed, but if the interviewer asked a question directly from one of us, we would answer for ourselves.

The American INS Agent was a white-haired man who looked to be in his sixties. He had specks that lay at the tip of his nose. He was a heavy-set man, and he was wheezing when he walked into the room we occupied. His interpreter was opposite what he was. The Pakistani interpreter was a young man in his thirties. He was as thin as a waif. He looked almost as if he were sick, but when he spoke he was very articulate—he enunciated his every word quite precisely.

As soon as these two took seats facing the six of us, the fidgeting among the members of the Monis family began. This was a nerve-jolting experience.

Looking directly at us, the Agent asked his first question, "Why do the six of you deserve to go to the U.S. more than all the other families that we are interviewing today?"

Since this was a general question, Dauod responded, "We might or might not deserve it more or less. We want to make something of ourselves. That is the main reason we deserve to go to the U.S. I have heard that it is the land of opportunities."

Dauod probably thought that he had done well and answered the question the way the majority of people would not. I was wondering how many times this Agent might have heard this answer. He was a stoic man, and Dauod's response did not elicit any kind of emotion from him.

He asked all of us questions—some general and some specific.

He asked me what I would offer America if I got there.

"All I can offer is what I have here." I pointed to my head indicating my wits.

The old man upon hearing this smiled. I guess he was not a stoic man after all.

The interview only took about thirty minutes, but it seemed like an eternity.

On the way back to the apartment in the cab, all six of us had our own take on how the interview had gone. No one really said that we did horrible, but none of us said that we were awesome either. The consensus was that we had done just well enough. The only sure answer to how well the interview had gone would be answered in about six weeks. That was when the official word would arrive form the U.S. via the U.S. Embassy in Pakistan of whether we were granted asylum into the U.S. or not. We would have to wait and see.

~ Chapter Twelve ~

The Big News

By the time the news arrived of whether we would go to the U.S. or stay in Pakistan, a lot had taken place in my life. I had been promoted from the third grade that I started to fifth grade. The principal seemed especially proud when he told me that me I would be able to skip the fourth grade and go directly to fifth. I assume that he believed it was the superior education that his school provided which enabled me to skip, but that was not the case. Fifth grade was okay. I again adjusted well to it although the majority of my friends were in the fourth grade.

Fifth grade was not bad. It was a review of things I had learned in the past. The one thing that was different and made it a bit tougher was that our science book was in English. I don't know why that was the practice across the schools in Pakistan, but we were to memorize phrases like, "Cell is the basic unit of all living things," and "All living things are made of cells."

I remember clearly the day we began memorizing those phrases. It was a nice day, and we had class outside. The only problem was that the science teacher who was forcing us to memorize these phrases failed to translate these phrases to Urdu for our understanding. Nonetheless that was the practice at that school.

In the late summer of 1988 the news arrived from the American Embassy. It was a very awkward moment as Dauod took the letter and ripped it open. All eyes were on him. He opened up the folded sheet of paper he found within. It had an official seal of the U.S. government to show that it was the "Real McCoy." He began reading it as well as he could. Among the Monis family at this point in time, I had the most knowledge of the English language having gone to school continuously. The letter was a letter of congratulations where the U.S. was welcoming us into the country.

The main point of the letter was that there was more red tape to go through. We had to report once again to the Embassy in order to get the paper work done for the travel to the U.S. There would be a period of a few months during which the whole process would be completed.

So we went to the Embassy a few times over the next few weeks and we got the paperwork done. At the other end of this process in America, Nadir was doing the same. He had to sign documents in which he gave his guarantee that the members of the Monis family who arrived in the U.S. would be provided for upon entering and would not be a burden on the U.S. government.

Amidst all the hectic run around, I celebrated my twelfth birthday on October 7th of 1988. That was a month before we were set to leave the country of Pakistan. Our trip would begin on November 25, 1988. We would arrive in the states on November 28, 1988. There were only a few errands we had to perform before the trip took place.

~ Chapter Thirteen ~

Journey into Paradise

Our trip began at mid-noon on the day we left Pakistan. Once again it was hard to leave the few friends that I had made. Most of them had come over to say goodbye this time though, which was a nicer way to leave than I had done previously in Afghanistan.

It was quite an emotional time for me, as all my friends brought me gifts. That year pocket sized comics were in vogue among people our age. I got a variety of titles to read. My closest friend gave me a mini piano. The factor that makes all these situations memorable and important are two-fold. On the one hand, these gifts showed that they cared; on the other hand, they are still a reminder for me of the friends I made in the span of a year that I lived in Pakistan. I still have the comics as well as the little toy piano. That is how much I have valued those gifts.

As for the rest of the Monis family, they were happy to be finally able to make the last leg of the journey they had begun three years before. The harsh part of it was that Mom was not able to come with us. I was only twelve, and being the baby of the family, I had always had Mom look after me, and be around me, so it was tough to leave her behind. In fact, it was hard for all of us. We had always been a family that stayed together and did things together, but now we were going to be thousands of miles apart. Additionally, Nabi, Sarah, and her kids could not join us either. This added to the emotional baggage that we were going to take with us to the United States. But I have learned that most journeys we take in life are bittersweet.

We traveled from the city of Islamabad to the Southern tip of Pakistan. This part of the trip took about half a day as we sat in our PIA (Pakistan International Airlines) plane. We landed in Karachi Airport at about six in the evening. As the trip progressed though, I lost track of time as well as day and night. We passed through so many time zones that it was tough to keep track of time. The last period during which I was actually able to log time was the trip from Karachi to Bangkok. We arrived in Bangkok at about two in the morning, but that night proved to be a long night. The next destination from Bangkok was Tokyo, Japan.

The plane was about an hour late, and when it got to the Bangkok Airport in Thailand, it was boarded immediately by all of the impatient passengers. We were off to go to Tokyo. This trip should have been the most exciting thing that had ever taken place in our lives, but the trip was becoming mundane quickly. Tiredness had taken over most of us as we either took naps or lazily glanced at the in-flight film that was playing. Most of us did not even have the strength to put on the earphones we were provided in order to listen to the dialogue the characters on the screen were involved in.

The trip was just about to get longer. When we finally arrived in Tokyo Airport, we were told that the flight, which was to take us to San Francisco, was late. The personnel at the airport did not know when this plane would arrive, therefore all the travelers whose destination was San Francisco,

USA were asked to stay in the lobby of the terminal. The Japanese personnel were quite pleasant as they patiently calmed some of the business travelers who seemed impatient. In particular, there was a man who was dressed in a high priced suit. He was complaining loudly about the flight, but the fact that I knew very little English, I could not decipher all that he said. But he was quite upset over the fact that there was no precise answer as to what time the plane would arrive.

We waited in the terminal for five hours. It was night when we got to Tokyo, and it was still night when we left Tokyo. I took a couple of hours' worth of naps in the uncomfortable chairs that covered the terminal lobby. All my brothers and sisters did the same as well. Dauod and Hamayoon also would walk the corridors of the terminal every once in a while. I did the same to copy the other male members of my family.

Finally the plane arrived. We boarded it, and we were almost in America. I sat by the window because I wanted to be able to get the first glimpse of paradise as we arrived in it. The trip was long and boring, and before long I lost interest in the darkness that blanketed the earth. I could not see the earth below because the Pacific Ocean was below a thick line of clouds above which hovered our plane. Every once in while, there would be a little break in the line of clouds and momentarily the earth below would appear. However, as if it was a dream or a mirage it would disappear again and darkness would encircle the plane once again.

When our plane landed in San Francisco, it was still nighttime. I had not seen daylight for a while now and I longed for some sunlight to shine, but that would have to wait until the next day. We were now very close to our final destination. Only one more flight remained before the family would be in San Antonio, Texas.

This plane ride was the most exciting one for me because we were about to be free. Ah, the word itself sounded so awesome as I repeated it to myself. Freedom! Freedom! I envisioned myself flying into the land of freedom. It was what my young mind had envisioned heaven to be. I was about to be there—we were all about to be free. We would be able to pursue whatever education we desired. We would be able to fulfill our dreams. I glanced at their faces, although jet-lagged, as we all were, there was a glow to the faces that looked back at me. They had the same smiles on their faces as I did.

The plane touched down in San Antonio International airport at 10:30 P.M. on November 28th, 1988. As I walked down the steps of the plane, I stopped momentarily to look at the sky above. Then I took in the sights and sounds of the city. It was sort of fitting that we arrived at night, because the beauty of America that I had seen on television in Afghanistan was always displayed at night. Just like those pictures on TV, this place was like the paradise I had envisioned. Why Texas, and why San Antonio? Some wonder. Nadir might have picked this town to reside in because of the various John Wayne movies that he had seen. In fact I myself could not wait to meet some of these cowboys. Climbing down the plane that night, the theme from any of John Wayne's films would be the perfect, most harmonious soundtrack for our journey.

We were alive and we had made it to paradise. Our journey of peril had taken us from the brink of death to the beauty of heaven. I closed my eyes as I gathered myself. This was almost overwhelming. This was going to be the place I would call home from now on. I took a deep breath and descended down the steps.

I wondered how much different my brother Nadir might look from his picture. I had not even seen my two nephews: Yosuf and Timur, and my niece Vanessa. How would my sister-in-law be? She was an American, what did that mean? Would she look, act, and feel differently? I was excited, all these overwhelming questions would be answered in a few hours. We were about to embark on a new life. The freedoms we dreamed of were now within our grasps. Dreams do come true. Paradise is within everyone's reach.

A Note to the Reader

This book was hard to complete because I had to relive many of the unpleasant experiences that I had gone through. There were so many things that happened in such a short period of time. As you know, if you have already read the book, remembering it all was somewhat of a painful experience. However, now that I have finished writing it, I am glad that I took the time to put these situations down on paper. Recently there has been a bit of animosity toward Afghans that some Americans have expressed. I believe this book has a universal human face that shows no matter where you come from and what may be your background, it is the human spirit that is strong in all societies and all cultures. I hope you enjoyed reading this book. I know that there are some questions that remain unanswered. I promise you that in the continuation of this story, the upcoming *Life in Paradise: A Family's Struggles*, your questions will be answered. I will tell you what happened to those who were still in Pakistan at the end of this book. I will also inform you on what happened to my brother Saleh and his family who stayed behind in Afghanistan. Additionally you will find out what happened to my uncles and cousins. I am fortunate to have found readers like you. Remember that America is a strong place, and its strength lies in its diversity. I hope to have you read more stories about the triumph of the human spirit.

M. Haroon Monis

11/27/01

Additional copies of this book may be purchased at

http://www.lulu.com/haroonmonis

Now available as well is the collection of short stories by Haroon Monis: *An Eternity and After in Hell and Other Stories*. Please turn the page to read an excerpt.

An Eternity and After in Hell

"Welcome to Hell," the hideous beast hissed.

With a smirk on my face I rose to my feet and found my stature well above that of the gatekeeper's. His clothing was nothing less than Gothic. Seeing him reminded me of the punkish-looking transients that I encountered while living in Austin, Texas. Nevertheless, he was not taken aback and offered no signs of obeisance; much to my dismay he chuckled to himself, as he looked me over. The pretentious glare in his eyes made me wonder whether I was going to be outwitted and overpowered. The oddness of the situation brought to mind my readings of *Alice in Wonderland*. I pondered what the little blonde pubescent would do or say in such a predicament. It was all I could do not to laugh at the absurdity of my life and now this. Then that little voice somewhere inside my head began to bring to mind those mad creations of such authors as Dean Koontz, Clive Barker, and Stephen King, turning my mind sour as I conjured up the outcomes of what such situations would bring. The cold and calloused orchestrations of an author's somewhat deranged mind would surely bring no worse fate than that which awaited me on the other side of that Gate.

Pulling myself from the rather unpleasant daydream, I noticed the sinister stare of my adversary. I thought of those boys who had come to take my daughter "out." They had the exact same look in their eyes. Little bastards. Those beady eyes poured rage into my blood, and I found myself wanting to paint the gateposts with this creature's blood—whatever color it might be.

The Alcoholic Dogs

Ibrahim's father, Mustafa, was a religious man. He never missed any of the five prayers on any given day. He would also always go to the musjid for the Friday prayers. Sometimes he would drag Ibrahim along with him.

For as long as Ibrahim remembered, Mustafa had been the only parent figure in his life since his mother had passed away giving birth to him. Surprisingly, Mustafa had not remarried despite everyone's expectations. It seemed that Mustafa was much happier without women in his life. In fact, his buddies were the most influential people in his life. Ibrahim remembered of more than one incident where he was punished because he had failed to treat his father's buddies the way his father wanted them to be treated. Mustafa and his buddies had a ritual of getting together Friday nights for drinking. Of course, Mustafa supplied all of the alcohol. Ibrahim knew of the infamous, locked cabinet in which all of his father's beverages were kept. He additionally knew where the key was kept. There were over a hundred bottles of liquor in the cabinet.

Ibrahim was an ordinary kid in most ways, but his father sometimes thought of him as an adult who was trapped in a child's body. Ibrahim acted so mature for his age, kept to himself, and displayed an extremely high degree of self-control for a nine-year-old. His actions at times held his father in awe.

Father and son were not alike, but in one way. They both disliked following the norms of the society in which they lived. Mustafa drank and hung out a lot with his friends. Ibrahim liked the companionship of animals to friends. He often visited his neighbors to play with their cats and bird pets. However, his favorite animals were dogs, which caused a little problem because according to superstition, dogs were dirty animals, and those who kept them as pets were frowned upon. The superstitious legend said that Muhammad had petted a cat on the back of its head, and therefore, had forever engraved his finger marks on all cats. According to the interpretations of the people, this story suggested that The Prophet approved of cats, so most of their neighbors who had pets had cats.

Unfortunately, since no such legend existed about dogs and since dogs and cats are seen as opposites, most people thought that dogs were not supposed to be kept by humans as pets. But Ibrahim loved dogs. He had read about them, and he wanted to have one. So, he decided to ask his father, "Baba, can I have a dog?"

"Sure son," he said; he was reading the Q'uran at that moment. He shut the Book, and taking a deep breath, looked up at Ibrahim. "But of course you know you will have to take good care of it. You know the neighbors have cats, and if your dog kills their cats, there will be trouble."

Ibrahim's eyes were gleaming with joy, like the eyes of a dog in the darkness. His whole face lit up as he said, "Oh, Baba, I will take real good care of my dog, you will see."

The next day, father and son went to the pound to look for a dog. Ibrahim picked a black puppy. His father wanted him to pick a different color, but he insisted that this was the one he wanted.

He did take good care of the puppy. He bathed, fed, and loved it. But after a week, the puppy suddenly died. The morning when Ibrahim found him lying limply really upset him, but Mustafa consoled him and told him that it was God's will for this to happen. He also added that if he wanted, they could go get another one.

So, they made a second trip to the pound. This time Ibrahim picked a brownish red puppy. This time the animal's life duration was two weeks. Again, his father told him that it was God's will for this to happen. He said to Ibrahim that God took creatures away from this world because he had a better place for them to go.

The third time Mustafa and Ibrahim went to the pound, Ibrahim picked a white puppy. It was really pretty, and had little black spots all over it. Ibrahim didn't want this one to die so he bought a lock for the cage in which he had kept his other puppies at night. His father told him laughing that a lock could not stop God if it was meant for the puppy to die. Ibrahim, nonetheless, insisted on buying the lock. He would lock the puppy in its cage every night before he went to bed, and he would check first thing in the morning to see if his puppy was alive.

After the passage of about a week, one night just as he was about to nod off to sleep, he heard the knob on his door turn. He pretended to be asleep.

His father entered the room, and stood by his bed gazing at him for a while. Then, he took the key to the cage and left the room as quietly as possible. Ibrahim was trembling as he got out of his bed and gazed through his window at the cage that was outside. He saw his father open the cage and take the puppy into his arms. He began petting the puppy and held it close to his bosom for a long time, but when he replaced it in its cage, it was lifeless and limp.

Tears were rolling profusely down Ibrahim's cheeks as he returned to bed and pulled the covers over him. His father entered his room shortly, and replaced the key on the nightstand. After he had left the room, Ibrahim cried loudly.

The next morning, the result was the same. His father gave him the same line as before that this was God's will. Again, he suggested that they could go get another puppy, but Ibrahim refused this time.

That evening when Mustafa returned home from work, he discovered that every single bottle in his liquor cabinet was broken. He was furious and he yelled for Ibrahim to come to the room. He interrogated him, accusing him of breaking the bottles. Ibrahim said, "Baba, I had no idea you had alcohol in our house. I didn't even know that this cabinet was full of bottles. I don't know where the key is either." To himself he mumbled, "Maybe it was God's will for this to happen."

Mistake of Innocence

He was alone in his dorm, sitting in the middle of the room with tears rolling down his cheeks. He knew it was not right for a man to cry. He hadn't cried before except during his childhood, but what had happened tonight was grotesque, and he could no longer hold back the tears which had pushed their way to the tip of his eyes every time he had heard them call him names or make fun of his accent. Jim opened his eyes and looked at the television screen. He listened to the singer harmonizing the words with full compassion as more tears rolled down his cheeks.

The song was about the importance of one's homeland. To Jim right now the song made a lot of sense. He wished he were in his own country. Then he would not have to hear all the unkind things they said about him. If he were in his country, he would not be crying, and he would not have done what he just did. He didn't want to do it. He told the guy not to approach him with the gun. The guy didn't listen and approached him, and in a flash it all happened. He was here now, sitting and weeping and feeling sorry for what had happened.

He came to Jim and said, "Empty out your pockets, and give me all the money you got."

"I don't have any money with me. I never carry cash."

He made fun of Jim by twisting his visage and changing his voice to sound like Jim and repeated what Jim had just said. Then he continued, "It's your kind that has stunk up this country. We don't need you any of you. You come and take our land and go to our school and steal our jobs. I should kill you, you son of a bitch!"

This triggered Jim. He thought of all the things that had gone on in the past years. Since junior high he had listened to similar phrases being spoken to him. The one phrase which everyone loved and he detested was, "Love it or leave it!" Many people added a few curse words to the end of the phrase. All this pondering made Jim make a sudden move. He slapped the gun out of the guy's hand, and picked it up from the floor. He heard the guy pleading,"Please don't kill me. Please! You can keep all your money. Here I'll give you mine."

www.ingramcontent.com/pod-product-compliance
Lightning Source LLC
Chambersburg PA
CBHW021245280526
45784CB00005B/2247